Sex Education
A Parents' Guide

John Timpson

All booklets are published thanks to the generous support of the members of the Catholic Truth Society

CATHOLIC TRUTH SOCIETY
PUBLISHERS TO THE HOLY SEE

Contents

Acknowledgements

I am grateful to all those who have discussed this booklet with me or provided stories or ideas to include.

Sex education from the beginning

Is there any need for this guide to sex education for Christian parents? Surely matters are straightforward. Young people need to find out about the facts of life, and schools are expert at explaining things. So why not let the teachers provide all the lessons that are needed? Otherwise young people might pick up misleading advice, and (for instance) think you can always tell if you've contracted a sexually transmitted disease (STD), or that a girl can't get pregnant before her first period. This guide for Christian parents would then be short and to the point: step in only if what the school provides is inadequate.

But the Church teaches quite the opposite! The Church makes it clear that while other educators can assist parents in providing sex education, 'they can only take the place of parents for serious reasons of physical or moral incapacity'.[1] Has the Church lost its senses? Is this just another case of Pope Benedict saying that distributing condoms makes the AIDS epidemic worse? Surely it seems obvious that it is better to use a condom than to catch AIDS? And if this is so then someone needs to teach young people how to use a condom, and that's hardly something that you would expect a father or mother to do.

There is a clash of mindsets in evidence here. But you might remember that neither the Pharisees nor Jesus's own disciples could imagine a world without divorce (see Matthew 19). Jesus, however, took a different stance: 'What God has united, human beings must not divide'. In the face of his disciples' skepticism, Jesus insisted that someone who divorces his wife and marries another is guilty of adultery. The disciples thought it would be better to stay single in this case. Jesus, of course, was looking to God's original intentions for life before sin entered the world.

Part of our task in this booklet is to consider how God intends young people to grow into a mature understanding of their sexuality. There is more than what meets the eye in all of these matters. After all, there is good evidence that handing out condoms to an entire population *can* make the AIDS epidemic worse[2], and that school-based sex education has failed to prevent increasing rates of many STDs. But first of all we need to clarify the purpose of sex education – what is it for? How we answer this question makes a big difference, affecting who is best placed to offer it and how they should go about it.

What is it that fulfills us?

You tear off the wrapper, and place a chunk of chocolate in your mouth. One taste bud after another receives the hit. Or you load the latest game onto your computer, and encounter the thrill of ever higher scores as you master the game's workings. A certain buzz can come, also, when a friend expresses admiration for that skimpy dress or when a desire for someone else's company first begins to be fulfilled.

A cocktail of neuro-chemicals

Can we really expect young people to exercise self control when a pleasure that is yet more intense than any of these examples is in prospect? As parents we will all have appreciated the intensity of sexual passion, and its tendency to bear away the will. Can we expect to regulate such earthquakes inside our sons and daughters? The general consensus in our society is that it's not possible for young people to exercise self control, even in situations where they themselves will experience harm.

The scientific evidence, after all, is quite clear that physical and emotional health is best served by abstaining from sexual activity until one is in a place to commit to a single partner for an entire lifetime.[3] Sexually Transmitted Diseases are now easy to pick up. In the 1960s one only had to worry about occasional cases of gonorrhea and syphilis, infections you could treat with penicillin. But while rates of infection vary from setting to setting, the prevalence of STDs is now substantial, especially amongst adolescents. Many of the more serious STDs are viral, and these can typically only be suppressed rather than cured. There is varying scope for cancer, infertility, or damage to organs such as the heart and kidneys. And while the situation is more complicated in relation to mental health, connections are evident between promiscuity and depression, attempts at suicide, self harm and drug abuse. One recent study, for instance, has shown that adolescents who have been sexually active experience significantly increased rates of depression and attempts at suicide, with the rates increased if drinking and smoking are added.[4]

An obvious thing to do is to try and ameliorate the consequences: hence 'safe' sex. But is handing out advice to 'put on a condom' or 'keep down the number of your sexual partners' really the best we can do for our sons and daughters? About a thousand women now die of cervical cancer each year in the UK alone, cancer that is almost always caused by high-risk strains of human papillomavirus (HPV). Studies indicate that you can reduce the chances of acquiring genital HPV infection by about one half through a consistent usage of condoms, but risk still remains. Of course, most sufferers will only end up with a wart, but that is no consolation if it is your son or daughter that has ended up with the cancer.

We can approach matters from another angle. The consequences of promiscuity go beyond the risks of personally contracting a sexually transmitted disease. Dopamine is a hormone released in the brain when we do anything exciting. It is something that one's body likes to be repeated. One of the most effective of all ways to stimulate dopamine release is through sexual activity.[5] We then tend to seek yet more intense variants of the pleasure in question, as otherwise the buzz from dopamine begins to fade.

But there are consequences if securing the next hit matters more than anything else. The genuine good of oneself and of others takes a back seat. When your focus is on your own desires, it is easy to pass on an STD or contribute to the formation of self-mutilating behaviour in someone else. Freda Bush tells of one young woman who attended a clinic in Mississippi, to find out that she had herpes.[6] The girl broke down into angry tears, although she eventually accepted that this was her situation. But she made it clear before she left the clinic that she would be unable to tell any future sexual partner of her condition. Her sense of shame was so great that she would be ready to infect someone else rather than disclose her infection.

Oxytocin, meanwhile, is a hormone that is relevant for women. Its release is stimulated by intimate skin-to-skin contact and by orgasm, as well as by the onset of labour and by stimulation of the nipples. Release of oxytocin provides a central reason why a mother becomes deeply attached to her new-born baby, or a girl to her sexual partner. The associated feelings of bonding and trust have a substantive neuro-chemical basis, reliant on the way that a woman's brain operates under the influence of oxytocin.[7] One study indicates that if a woman hugs her partner for at least 20 seconds then oxytocin is released in the brain.[8] Flannery O'Connor provides a compelling example of the effect of oxytocin in her short story *Good Country People*. A travelling Bible salesman calls, and a young woman, Hulga, decides to seduce him. What she isn't quite able to predict is the effect that an extended kiss is to have on her own attitude to a man she had planned to dismiss after a little pleasure.

The comparable hormone that operates in men is vasopressin. When a man has extended physical contact with a woman it also results in bonding on his part, although the effect of this neuro-chemical is not as well understood as that of oxytocin. Greater release is again stimulated through sexual intercourse.

Sexual activity provides a compelling experience of connectedness for both men and women. But these bonding mechanisms can become damaged through taking on multiple sexual partners and through repeated bad experiences. This makes it more difficult to bond in the future. The brain adapts and changes in response to experience, and this has consequences for the rest of one's life. These neuro-chemicals help to explain why break-ups can be painful for both men and women, although this seems to be especially the case for women given the effect of oxytocin. Our bodies are designed for a long-term relationship with a single partner.

A wedding night

But does the Church simply offer a diagnosis of 'here lies death'? Are we destined to a life of ultimately frustrated desires whichever way we turn, as pleasure meets its natural limits? Is there no scope for substantive happiness lasting an entire lifetime for our sons and daughters?

Pope John Paul II took a particularly keen look in his own teaching at the account of a wedding night in the Bible. The Book of Tobit tells a strange story. Sarah had married seven times already. On attempting to consummate the marriage, each husband had been killed by a demon. Her cousin Tobias then turned up on a quest for his father's silver, and asked for her hand in marriage. Sarah's father, Raguel, could not refuse, as Tobias' request was backed up by the full force of the Jewish Law. Raguel was so worried that his new son-in-law would meet the same fate as the others that he had his servants dig a grave in the middle of the night. Had not Tobias fallen head-over-heels in love with her, so that his heart no longer belonged to himself? Why should they not rush straight into each others' arms on entering the marriage chamber?

What if your son were in a similar situation? He falls for a stunning girl, who has become deeply attached to him; and they find themselves in a situation where there is every inducement to follow the natural course of their desires. Do we really expect two young people to resist each other's advances simply because they don't have a condom to hand?

Something, though, was different this time around. When a servant girl went in on them later in the night, both Sarah and Tobias were still alive. What was it, then, that enabled Tobias to survive? Pope John Paul drew particular attention to the way that Tobias calls Sarah 'my sister'. For the Pope this meant that Tobias genuinely looked to take Sarah's good into account. Tobias did not seek to dominate his wife for his own pleasure or convenience, but in this respect treated her as a sister. He possessed a self-mastery that enabled him to act with the good of his wife keenly in mind. Tobias knew that given her marital history they must first of all pray to God before laying down together for the night.

The implication is that those earlier husbands had taken Sarah as his wife in a spirit of lust. They must each have experienced an urgent desire to take her straight to bed, heedless of the potential consequences for both themselves and her. One might think that these seven husbands each had a right to consummate their marriage, but the story suggests that even the act of consummating one's marriage needs to be integrated into a wider understanding of what is good for us.

Education for chastity

We need an appreciation of the different good things that are linked to our sexuality. Sexual intimacy with another person can indeed be beneficial. It can give one the zest to face life or provide the glue to help a married couple to stay together. But the story of Tobias and Sarah reminds us that other things matter as well. And if other good things exist that are linked to our sexuality, perhaps we might be able to help young people choose them? Sex education is not simply about giving out information as to how human sexuality operates, a user's manual concerned with producing the fewest ill effects. Perhaps, after all, there is scope for other approaches to sex education than just minimising the consequences of promiscuity?

The virtue of chastity, indeed, is all about retaining one's capacity to act for the good of others in the face of sexual desire.[9] It might not be a fashionable word in medical or educational circles generally, but chastity remains essential if one is to act for the good of others. Education for chastity is not so much about developing the strength of the will to resist the fiercest of temptations, but rather the capacity to order one's entire life around what is good. We need a keen appreciation that there are things to give and receive that might outweigh the satisfaction in prospect from sexual intimacy with another person. In this booklet we will explore how to pass on to our sons and daughters a way of life that brings them deep fulfillment. There is a glimmer of light as to why parents need to take charge.

Fathers and mothers taking a lead

Let us go back to the beginning of Tobias and Sarah's story. Tobias' father, Tobit, was a Jewish exile in Nineveh. It was bad enough to live amongst a people who disdained his customs, but his fellow Jews, too, had begun to eat food that the Law of Moses forbade. He alone stood out from the crowd, burying the dead bodies of his fellow countrymen. On one occasion he buried the bodies of some Jews who the King of Assyria had killed. Tobit was spotted, and had to flee for his life. After a change of King, he returned penniless to the city.

The story tells us that, not long after this, his son Tobias came back with a report that a Jewish person had been strangled, and his body lay abandoned in the market place. Off Tobit went to dig a grave, and bury the man's body. Not surprisingly his neighbours poured scorn on him, as if he had not learnt that burying the dead could lead him to no good: "Once before he had to flee, yet here he is again, beginning to bury the dead." (*Tb* 2:8) But Tobias knew his father would wish to bury the body, and he now found himself drawn after his father's example. Tobit, certainly, had been ready to speak his mind to his son. The Bible even records a lecture where Tobias was told to do good works whenever he could, pay his servants promptly, not get drunk, and so on. But it is not so much Tobit's advice that is of interest to us, as much as his example in standing out from the crowed.

A parents' witness

How you live as a father or mother makes a difference. What are some of the lessons that one's offspring might learn, for instance, if you are cohabiting rather than married? Well, right from the start there is the message that sexual relations need not be kept within marriage. But one might well also pass to a son or daughter the expectation that his or her own sexual unions will be short-lived. It is now well known that cohabitations are far more fragile than marriages, and that it is much more likely that one or both partners will be conducting additional sexual liaisons beyond their relationship. Another lesson one's offspring is likely to learn is that convenience trumps the substantive good of others in sexual matters. Convenience, after all, is the effective reason most often given for cohabiting rather than marrying, whether on financial, legal, social, sexual or other grounds. But what of the consequences that come to the children when a relationship breaks down, or of the increased risk of physical and sexual abuse to children within cohabitations? What of the studies showing that aggression is at least twice as common among cohabitors as it is among married partners,[10] and rates of depression for women in cohabiting relationships are at least three times higher than those for married women?[11]

While each cohabiting relationship is in itself unique, and any one couple may stay together for their entire lives, some underlying factors are evidently at work. Cohabitations are intrinsically based on a more restricted form of commitment than that present in marriage. Studies point out that cohabiting couples typically spend less time together in comparison to married couples,[12] possibly offering reduced scope for the bonding effect of oxytocin and vasopressin. One can become accustomed to a high level of independence within a relationship, so that the needs of one's partner are not so straightforwardly at the forefront of one's mind. The upshot is that even if you manage to find a satisfying lifelong cohabitation, the chances are not good that this will be the case for your offspring.

Cohabitation provides one good example of how a parent's own witness in sexual matters influences one's children, but there are plenty of other examples. Reserving sexual intercourse for a lifelong marital relationship, by contrast, helps to build a deeper and more enduring union for the couple themselves, with the effects spilling over to the children of the marriage. The children of such a couple are more likely to receive an inside view on the possibility of reconciling their sexuality with what satisfies over the long term. The witness of choosing to stay faithful to your husband or wife, or to living a chaste life as a single parent cannot be underestimated. The Church calls this witness of the parents 'the most valid basis for educating children in love'.[13] You cannot pass on what you do not have yourself.

Chatting to your son or daughter

The methods used in sex education should match the aims. A couple who are considering getting married will need to be able to talk intimately together about sexual intercourse, as will a married couple. Dialogue in an intimate, one-to-one setting represents a baseline for any form of sex education. It is no surprise that we see Tobias talking to his new wife about how best to express their sexuality together. And where better to begin to learn this capacity than through engaging in discussion with a parent? The Church reminds us that sexuality 'is oriented towards interpersonal dialogue';[14] it finds its place within a communion of persons. If the intention is to learn how to develop and sustain an intimate relationship, then it is hard to see how this particular aim can be easily advanced nowadays through sex education in the public realm of a classroom. A mixed setting of girls and boys allows vast scope for ribald comments, whether right there in the classroom or later in the playground.

Dialogue on intimate sexual matters between a son or daughter and parent, though, rarely happens of its own accord. The parent will usually need to initiate conversation. The most straightforward time to begin this as a parent is when the physical changes associated with puberty become apparent, occurring as this does when young people typically begin to take more initiative in how they lead their own lives. The Church indeed indicates that children are in the years of innocence until puberty begins: "This period of tranquility and serenity must never be disturbed by unnecessary information about sex."[15]

The physical changes of puberty usually begin to emerge between 9 and 11 for girls, and between 10 and 13 for boys, as hormones are released into the body. A girl may first of all become moody, and experience greater body odour and vaginal discharge, before the budding of one or both breasts or the appearance of pubic hair. The first menstrual cycle then typically occurs a couple of years or so after the appearance of breast buds, at around 12 or 13. For boys, moodiness can occur early on before the testes become enlarged and the penis lengthens. It is only after the subsequent development of pubic hair that a boy's voice will deepen or increases in muscle mass occur.

Parents can take advantage of the natural curiosity that accompanies such physical change. Discussion focused at least initially around these changes provides one straightforward entry point. It can help to have a few questions ready to simulate conversation, rather than look to give a mini-lecture. 'You're beginning to grow much quicker now', or 'Have you seen this happening to your body? What do you think is going on?'

The variation in time at which these physical changes emerge is also accompanied by a variation in readiness on the part of the young person to discuss intimate personal matters, hence the teaching of the Church that the most intimate matters should be dealt with on a one-to-one basis.[16] Indeed, the Church proposes personal dialogue between parents and their children as the 'normal and fundamental method of sex education'.[17] The aim is to tailor discussion to the unique characteristics of your own son or daughter. One mother recalls: 'I have to give different answers to both of them, because one seems to understand very quickly, while the other wants to know everything in full detail.' Patience certainly is required: her boys can hear something one week, and have entirely forgotten it a couple of weeks later. But this isn't always the case, as she is also aware: 'One of my sons loves ketchup. He even had it on his ice cream once; ketchup with this, ketchup with that. One year he gave it up every day during Lent. He asked once if you were able to have children before you got married, and it occurred to me that there was a similarity with this experience of his. So I asked him, "Do you remember what is was like when you were able to have ketchup after waiting for it for all of Lent?" He knew that self denial really could lead to fulfillment. He had experienced this for himself. He knew how proud he was at the end of Lent. It's like ketchup after Lent – you appreciate it more in this way. The challenge here is to draw on his own experience, and his memories, so that this is something to which he can commit himself. This is your responsibility. This conversation was not something that he would forget a few weeks later, as he had done with some of our other discussion about his own anatomy.'

Fathers are the ones to talk to sons, and mothers to their daughters (although there will be some situations where this is not possible or realistic). Girls clearly will need more detail on the cycles of fertility, with more discussion for boys around the development of the genital organs. Discussion will in time also need to occur in time on the purpose and use of one's sexual powers, with attention also to what it means to be a mother or father, and indeed to be a virgin. But it will also help to discuss the effects of oxytocin and vasopressin, and where one can find fulfillment that lasts an entire lifetime.

A variety of triggers

Further considerations can also trigger conversations with a son or daughter, as one is aware of the way that he or she responds to those around them. One mother recalls that she was in the car, and some girls walked past dressed in short skirts. Her ten year-old gave them a good long gaze. She thought: 'He's paying attention to girls, and what they look like.' And a little later she recalls that he told his little sister, 'Get dressed, you're naked.' These incidents for her were a trigger to begin to his sex education. The extent to which one needs to introduce issues of immoral sexual practices and their consequences will also depend in part on what your son or daughter hears about from others. If certain subjects are avoided it may simply be the case that knowledge about them comes from peers.

Or your son or daughter, equally, could initiate discussion. Some children are naturally quite inquisitive, and can just keep on asking question after question. A younger child might well be able to wheedle rather a lot out of you, while an older child has hardly thought to ask. Or perhaps a question might come in response to something that a friend has said in the playground. Clearly in this case a parent will also need to respond, perhaps providing less explicit discussion with a younger child, but still addressing the immediate issue at hand or controlling obscene language. Or it might be that a television programme you have viewed together provides a lead into discussion about sexuality. Taking advantage of such natural triggers can help a young person to feel that their privacy has not been deliberately invaded. Perhaps a friend is getting married, or someone has had a baby. Books can also be helpful in triggering discussion, and help to lengthen a conversation so that it is not cut short by the first pause for thought. Teenage girls might be interested in Carmen Marcoux's novels *Arms of love* and *Surrender,* which take in such themes as courtship and discernment in the setting of the United States. Young people need to retain a measure of choice as to how and when they want to discuss things, so that dialogue is genuinely involved.

Making space

All of this assumes that a channel of communication is actually open. This means bearing patiently with our children's tantrums, moods, unresponsiveness and rudeness. Rather than reacting with anger or incomprehension we need to learn to find constructive charitable responses, even if we also impose other consequences or ask for an apology. If you do not have extended conversations with your son or daughter about other matters, it is hard to see how it will suddenly become natural to talk about these most intimate of matters. This requires time on the part of parents, and a willingness to sacrifice other things. Children's time, meanwhile, can easily be occupied by video games, social networking and so on. But if we really do desire to see something happen, then regular habits are hard to beat. One father has initiated a regular chat with his teenage daughter before she heads off to bed – time one-on-one becoming a regular feature of their relationship.

It might well take some reading beforehand to establish an initial level of confidence about all these things, although the recommendations in the appendix will help here. But if a parent displays a willingness to go away and find further things out, before returning to a conversation, then this can only indicate your willingness to act for your son or daughter's good. Concerns about one's own sexual history are perhaps more of a challenge. It is our present lives, though, that matter most of all in discussion with our children, as this is what is most evident to them and it reflects also our settled approach to life.

Society and sex education

While the parents' witness, conversation and approach to life matter a great deal, we all still live within a wider social setting. It is easy to overestimate the effect on behaviour arising simply from personal beliefs. Imagine a young person leaving their family and friends behind to start up an entirely new life on their own in a distant city. The relationships that they form early on will have a huge influence on their way of life as it emerges in this setting. And if all the available friends are out drinking and looking to each other for sexual pleasures, then the young person's beliefs are likely to shift.

It is not as if we can decide to live in a perfect world. Tobit could not simply have willed himself back to the land of Israel, under the rule of a perfect king, but he could still retain the customs of his people even in exile. And we, too, have choices to make about how we live our own lives, whether in the clothes we wear, the media that we consume, our drinking habits, our approaches to dating and so on.

Dealing with the media

Sexual images are increasingly prevalent in today's world, and not only in the media. Toys, clothes, games and so on aimed at children have all seen an increased use of sexual images in recent years.[18] This means taking an active interest in what our sons and daughters encounter. One particular challenge concerns the early sexualisation of girls, given the widespread use of sexualised images of girls and young women in fashion magazines, hip-hop music, films, advertising, merchandising, and the media at large; and then in the way that all these cultural references are endlessly reinforced through social interactions. The challenge is to find suitable alternatives. There is a need to search out good films, read reviews, watch material in advance, track down good books and so on.

You can't quite see teachers requesting permission to trawl through their pupils' social networking sites. Parents, though, can quite reasonably make it a condition of use that they also have access to what is posted up on MySpace, bebo, hi5, Facebook, Tagged or whatever. The aim would not be to post up your own comments for all to see, but rather occasionally to make reference to postings.

It's also important to monitor video games, and to install a filter on internet access to block pornographic sites or to install software to monitor internet usage. It is quite possible to access pornographic sites without intending to, simply by entering an incorrect version of a popular web address. It is said that the *average* age of a child's first exposure to internet pornography is 11 years old, and that 90% of all young people have viewed such pornography by the time they are 16 years old.[19] So it's best to ensure that things are in place before any problems emerge. Pornography constitutes a particularly powerful form of sex education. One young man, Steve, tells how he first came across pornography as a twelve year-old.[20] He soon became an addict, and increasingly came to see girls as objects to be used, and then discarded. He became quite uncomfortable around girls, blaming them for inflaming his own lusts. A sense of shame began to colour his entire life, and it was only when he heard that God had something better for him that he began to kick his habit.

Laying down the law

It will help to lay down some clear limits, even as one also tries to transmit responsibility. Take watching television or videos, for example. One approach is simply to allow your children to watch virtually anything. Sexual images, though, lodge in the mind, and one thought leads to the next. Simply making an occasional negative comment about 'inappropriate behaviour' is unlikely to dislodge the associated images. Television programmes that habitually glamorise sensual pleasure are simply best avoided. Children particularly need help in dealing with activities that have the potential for addiction, even if it is 'only' video games. A clear rule about 'when' or 'how much' can help a person go a long way in learning how to regulate potentially compulsive desires.

What about rules in relation to dating?

In the UK it is a common occurrence for 9 year olds to pair off with each other, but it is entirely reasonable to say, 'No dating while you are a young teenager living at home', 'No overnight stays in the family home with someone from the opposite sex', or 'You must be back by 11.00pm.' One friend tells how as a sixteen year-old she went out to a party, and was asked to be back by 10pm. She arrived home 20 minutes late, and the next time she asked to go to a party her parents said, 'No; you didn't do what you had said last time.' As you might expect, she hit the roof. She was complaining to one of her friends, who didn't quite see why she was so put out. 'You should consider yourself fortunate. My parents don't care if I'm out until two or three in the morning; at least your parents care for you.'

The balance, though, will shift as time goes on. It is hard, or almost impossible, to introduce new rules once you have established a pattern in life, or to suddenly start talking about personal issues when conversation is limited to passing the cornflakes. We are creatures of habit, and our readiness to seek certain pleasures becomes settled. It is not as if we are angels, holding our entire destiny in our hands at one point in time. Our bodies, hearts and minds all learn to respond in certain ways, and these don't shift simply because a parent has come to see things differently. Imagine a teenager who is already used to a significant amount of freedom, and then consider taking those freedoms away! And once a young person has left home, the chances of offering sex education diminish yet further.

Learning to bury the dead

It is not easy to help one's children stand out from their peers. Margaret tells how her fourteen year-old daughter, Olivia, received an invitation to a friend's party. Margaret assumed, perhaps naively, that it would be some sort of tea-time get-together in the friend's house, and said it would be fine for Olivia to go. She only took a closer interest when her daughter talked about buying a miniskirt and wearing it with leggings. Further investigation revealed that the party was in a public setting, and due to finish with taxis back home in the early hours of the morning. But the invitation had already been accepted, and 'all' Olivia's friends would be there. What should Margaret do?

Her first response was to talk to a few friends, and to her husband. A blanket refusal at this point would have been a real challenge. There had to be some other way. It was only after some extended heart-searching, and an initial determination that her daughter simply could not do this, that a realistic way out came to mind. A friend was summoned to help, whose daughter was a good friend of Olivia's. She agreed to send her over to stay for the weekend. This would give Olivia both compensation, and an excuse. The strategy worked well, as Olivia was much more worried about playing the hostess than about missing the party. We can only make significant demands of our children if we provide substantive assistance in the process.

How do you learn to stand out from the crowd? How would you support your daughter when all her friends scorn her for wearing a 'long skirt' or not having a boyfriend? This is one critical capacity for sex education in a world where pleasure is placed above the destiny of others. If as parents we are not first of all able to respond with firmness and imagination in response to such issues, then our youngsters in their turn are likely to succumb to the relentless social pressure on such issues. If certain clothes are off limits for being too immodest, then we need to help our teenagers find alternatives. They may cost more money, but our young people need to have a positive attitude towards their own bodies.

Rather than simply 'opt out', one route is to look for quirky alternatives that will still appeal to your son or daughter, and that their peers may still respect. One family is keen on purity rings. A purity ring is often marked with a symbol such as a cross, and is accompanied by making a promise to God to abstain from sexual intercourse before marriage. As one mother puts it: 'They announce to the world that you are different; they give a young person courage.'

Resilience and firmness

We also need to pass on a readiness to act with firmness. It's not only boys who can be predatory. One young lad turned up at secondary school to be told by a girl that he was now her boyfriend. She liked the look of him, and he was to be hers. She told everyone else in the class that this was the case, and others started repeating it to him as well. He found that he could do nothing in the face of her lies, and came home in tears. Young people need to realize that someone else might approach them simply as a source of pleasure, rather than with a concern for their good. One can easily realize this only too late, after the effects of dopamine, oxytocin or vasopressin have already kicked in.

A certain resilience is needed to reject an 'in your face' offer of sexual pleasure. Some knowledge also will be important as to the effects of drugs and alcohol, in both raising the sensibility for sexual pleasure and diminishing the capacity for self control. Ideally, one wants to avoid unpleasant situations in the first place, but young people also need to learn to look for active lines of defence, rather than to allow a situation to follow its 'natural' course.

Forming a Christian society

Any sex education worth its name will pay attention to the social setting within which someone lives his or her life. Friends are drawn to each other's values, whether in relation to which clothes to wear or which songs to listen to. Chastity only makes sense if there is a group of people who share much of their lives and values in common. In years gone by there was a strong sense of community in our parishes, with social clubs, sports teams, dances, charitable activity and much more besides. But this is now harder to find, as if religious devotion on its own is insufficient to sustain a Christian community. Without these wider activities, it is surely harder for Catholic young people to form friendships with each other.

We delude ourselves if we think that a chaste life is likely without a supportive social environment. Parents who are committed to their child's good will do what it takes also to help them find a suitable peer group. It might mean a move of houses, schools or parishes, or joining one of the new movements within the Church. Determination is required on the part of the parent. Sex education in this case might mean reorganising life rather than hoping that things will work out. There is a Biblical story that tells something of the pressures at work here. Abraham's nephew, Lot, moved with his two young daughters to a remote location. There were no young men around, and in time the two daughters decided to have children by their own father. They managed to get Lot drunk one night, and the rest is history. Lot ruled out any possibility for his daughters to find husbands; and it is no surprise that they reacted against their situation.

It is fascinating that sex education was critical to the establishment of the Jewish nation. The Jewish nation is most definitively identified with Jacob, as the father of the twelve tribes. All of his sons remained within the community. One of the more immediate reasons why Isaac was not the founder of a great nation was because he was not able to educate both of his sons in their sexuality. After he had lost his blessing as the first born son, Easu deliberately searched out a pagan wife in order to offend his father. But Jacob himself conducted his sexual relations in a way that was subordinate to his faith, marrying within his own community. While Jacob's sons weren't exactly perfect, something had shifted.

It is hard to imagine a world without promiscuity, STDs, infidelity and divorce. But none of this is inevitable, and as parents we can do a great deal to help our children avoid such scourges. Complaining about the actions of others usually serves little purpose – what we need to do rather is shape our own lives and actions to serve our children's destinies. God has given each of us a responsibility to take the initiative, rather than just leave events to run their course.

Others eager to give sex education

Thus far we have primarily focused on ways for parents to educate their sons and daughters. But schools, health authorities, careers advisors and politicians also display an interest in sex education. They do have the capacity to be supportive of your role as a parent, but any of these groups may instead bring a quite different agenda with them.

Other educators can assist

Schools provide a critical social environment for our children, and are increasingly also the partner most likely to intervene in relation to sex education. It will help to pull together some of the teachings of the Church on the respective responsibilities of schools and parents.

Schools and other educators are *not* simply supposed to take over: 'The assistance of others must first and foremost be given to parents rather than to their children.' Schools take the lead with children in virtually every other area, setting the agenda and the terms of engagement, so something of a change of mindset is required in order to remain faithful to this teaching. For instance, in some Catholic schools it is the parents who are provided with resources to use with their sons and daughters. The school itself does not provide sex education directly to pupils, but rather assists the parents. It is then quite reasonable for the school to host occasional inspirational speakers on chastity, as a supplementary means of sex education. Nor are parents actually required by the Church to accept what help the school might wish to offer: 'If parents believe themselves to be capable of providing an adequate education for love, they are not bound to accept assistance.'[21]

The Church is clear that parents are able to provide what is needed in a way that schools, or even chastity educators, cannot: 'Each child is a unique and unrepeatable person and must receive individualised formation.' 'Each child's process of maturation as a person is different. Therefore the most intimate aspects, whether biological or emotional, should be communicated in a personalised dialogue.' 'Parents are well aware that their children must be treated in a personalised way, according to the personal conditions of their physiological and psychological development, and taking into due consideration the cultural environment of life and the adolescent's daily experience.'[22] It is challenging for other educators to provide individualised formation and personalised dialogue on any subject, let alone on something so sensitive as sex education; hence the *requirement* to assist parents in the first instance.

A sense of privacy

One of the Church's key concerns is that sex education must respect each young person's sense of privacy and modesty. Sex education in other settings 'must not include the more intimate aspects of sexual information, whether biological or affective, which belong to individual formation within the family'.[23] This teaching of the Church would evidently rule out sex education beyond the family that involves young people commenting on sexual desires and relationships that they have themselves experienced, or discussing the actual stage of development of their own sexual organs. It rules out other educators from addressing such intimate territory.

Interactive elements to any form of sex education provide a real challenge: 'No one should ever be invited, let alone obliged, to act in any way that could objectively offend against modesty or which could subjectively offend against his or her own delicacy or sense of privacy'.[24] Graphic portrayals of information on the physical aspects of human sexuality can also harm this sense of personal privacy and modesty, even in cartoon form, as can erotic dramatic performances (something that the Church also rules out from all forms of sex education).[25] If the intention is for sex education to help a young person establish a lifelong and exclusive relationship with someone of the opposite sex, then one needs to learn how to retain this sense of privacy before others.

Situated within a secular world

Many programmes of education in sex and relationships do simply concentrate on handing over information to pupils, such as how to minimise one's chances of getting an STD or avoid pregnancy. But it is clear that knowledge on its own provides only a limited basis for action. The research evidence, for instance, is clear that how much one knows about HIV or AIDS only has a modest effect on whether one actually uses a condom: 'Perceived vulnerability to infection with HIV/AIDS, worry or fear of infection, and perceptions of the seriousness of infection all had small average correlations with intentions to use condoms.'[26] A review published in *The Lancet* suggests that condom use may increase the occurrence of STDs as they give a false sense of security and can lead more people to become sexually active.[27] In a similar fashion, it is clear that widespread availability of the morning after pill makes no impact on rates of pregnancy or abortion.[28]

It is also the case that some programmes of sex education sideline or contradict Catholic moral teaching. One commonly used set of videos shows sexual intercourse as a normal activity between people in a 'relationship', making no mention of marriage. The video for 10 year olds states that masturbation is perfectly morally acceptable, as are sexual relationships between those of the same sex. Another video for 6 year olds shows a clitoris/penis, commenting that contact can 'feel nice' and that this sensation is perfectly normal. This may be, factually correct, but it ignores any moral context. Or a programme may simply assume that it is not possible for a young person to live chastely in the face of erotic drives or may present human sexuality as an extension of animal behaviour.

A mother recalls being surprised that children in a Catholic primary school were given sex and relationships education, but the head-teacher and parish priest assured her that it was all in the context of Church teaching. She assumed that the professionals must know best and that it was good for children to be taught it at school: 'I put down my gut reservations to my parental ignorance. But as my daughter finished the first year in primary school, I asked the head-teacher to lend me the videos. The second year pupils were due to have their first tranche of sex and relationships education. We didn't get around to looking at them until the day before the end of summer holiday, when we had to return them. The videos followed the format and production standards for schools TV for the relevant age-groups spanning 5-11year-olds over six videos. Most of the material seemed innocuous, but it was interspersed with short sections of cartoons showing very adult material with calm backing music and a soothing voice-over.'

In all of this there is no hard and fast distinction between what is taught and how it is taught. Who it is who teaches makes a difference as well. Take a teacher who is utterly convinced that his or her pupils need to know how to use condoms. Is it reasonable to expect them to put across the teaching of the Church on contraception as true? After all, less than half of teachers in Catholic secondary schools in England and Wales are themselves Catholic, and surveys indicate that only a modest proportion of Catholics accept this teaching any longer. But the Church indicates: 'Those who are called to help parents in educating their children for love must be disposed and prepared to teach in conformity with the authentic moral doctrine of the Catholic Church.'[29]

The pressure on Catholic schools from a secular culture can be intense, even simply through 'high-quality' resources that are offered for modest or no cost. Schools are highly susceptible to funding pressures, and increasingly driven by the targets that authorities set. If the services of a school nurse are free, then it will come as no surprise that many schools will take up the offer. But what if the nurse is obliged to offer a full range of contraceptive services or facilitate abortion? Church law is clear that any Catholic whose assistance is essential to an abortion is automatically excommunicated.[30]

It is hardly surprising that there is limited, if any, evidence for the effectiveness of sex education in schools. An editorial in the *British Medical Journal* reported 'Most studies on sex education programmes in schools examine intermediate outcomes only, such as pupil satisfaction or reported condom use. This often facilitates premature and false claims of success, whereas more robust outcome measures such as rates of terminations, unplanned conceptions, and sexually transmitted infections show no benefit.'[31] By contrast, there is good evidence for sex education involving parents.[32]

Taking the initiative

Given this picture, it would surely be unreasonable to assume that people in authority know best, and to not inquire further. You need substantive reasons to believe that your child's innocence or modesty will be respected, and this needs to be combined with a recognition that people are inclined to tell you what they feel you want to hear. The only way to test the reality is actually to find out what will be taught, who will teach it, and how it will be taught. Courage may be required even to find out what is going on, as in practice a school may not actually consult with parents on the sex education they are to offer.

One is then in a position to act in a way that is good for a son or daughter, as this couple recall: 'Knowing that our 11 year-old daughter was going to secondary school and would be given the full details of sexual intercourse in her biology lessons, we used the best materials we could find that presented sex education from a Catholic perspective, and took her through the details as delicately as we could. Even so, she was not happy to hear it and found it distasteful. She still didn't like the subject when she covered it in biology. I asked if she preferred hearing about it from mum, but she replied that she didn't like hearing about it from any source. She mentioned that some of the other girls also found it unpleasant, but most of the rest were not bothered as they had covered it in primary school.' The family would rather have addressed matters in their own time, but decided to anticipate some of what would be covered.

Certainly if a look at the curriculum, methods or teachers indicates that misconceptions are likely to be put forward, one can discuss these directly with the son or daughter. One parent, after securing a copy of the resources to be used, noticed a consistent strain. The programme consistently presented human sexuality through discussion of animals. It applied moral language to the behaviour of animals, emptying this language of its substantive content. In what sense do animals care for each other? But seeing any of this depends upon you taking an interest in the first place, in securing and reading the materials in advance.

Another option is simply to withdraw your son or daughter from planned lessons. Classroom lessons can give rise to lasting impressions or attitudes that are hard to dispel. One should communicate with the school, perhaps indicating that your child will not be attending on the days when the said lessons are to occur. You would also need to prepare your son or daughter for any such step. One mother simply told her son that he was 'going to learn this a different way; because I'm best placed to teach this to you, and doing it this way will be good for us.' Perhaps also it might help to rehearse with your son or daughter what they might say to their friends. This could teach the lesson that if something matters to us then we need to act, rather than to complain and do nothing. Or it might help your child to realise that in this area they need to stand apart somewhat from their peers. What matters above all are concrete means and actions that actually put first what is good for your son or daughter.

It would certainly be possible to say: 'The Church says it ought to be this way, so please change the lessons my child is to receive.' In a fallen world, though, we are not simply able to enforce our rights, even in cases where the Church teaches something *must* be a certain way. And this is true whether the person failing to respond to the just request is a classroom assistant or head-teacher. What of the school that has just spent several thousand pounds on a curriculum – are they likely to throw away all the materials just because one parent thinks they aren't up to scratch? You are not under an obligation to start a campaign at your local school to dispense with a school nurse who is promoting abortions, but you can take steps to warn off your child or to move schools. In such situations all that one can do is take the initiative in love, acting above all for the good of one's own children.

God has answered your prayers

Esau came back from hunting one day, famished. How fortunate, then, that his brother Jacob had just made some soup. The aroma filled his senses – he could almost feel it hitting his belly. He had to have that soup. The story is, of course, well known. For the sake of a small pleasure Esau gave up an entire lifetime of blessing. He scorned the gifts that only God could give him, preferring instead a pot of soup.

It is easy to look down on Esau, but easy also to follow his example. We need to learn to value the gifts that God alone can give us. When Esau discovered after all that a blessing was worth having, it was too late. He had already chosen to live a way of life that ranked sensual pleasure above blessing. Jacob, by contrast, was ready to value something that concerned his future life. It is this, indeed, that marks him out as the father of the Jewish nation.

And indeed it was good

What then of the good things which are associated with human sexuality? Bodily health, certainly, needs to be respected in any consideration of sexuality. As human beings with bodies, sexual intercourse serves human reproduction. The reproductive function of sexual intercourse in this way opens up the possibility of life as a family together, with varied scope for love and mutual generosity. But powers of fertility cannot be evoked at will. It is essential that sex education enables young people to appreciate that one might lose this possibility to confer life on another. Smoking, for instance, may dramatically lower one's fertility, so that those who smoke while young might lose some sense of their connection to the future. Many sexually transmitted diseases lower or destroy fertility. To 'take a risk' on catching an STD is to disdain one's capacity to be generous to others. The choices here might not be made quite so deliberately, but they are real nonetheless.

Our sexual powers allow the possibility of bonding with someone else for an entire lifetime. As human persons we are constituted in relationship with others. A deep and enduring unity with someone else represents a fundamental element of what we find satisfying as human persons. There is a completeness that we desire in our most intimate relationships, something first learnt at our mother's breast. The desire for unity with another is stronger even than the desire for pleasure, something to which countless divorces give testimony. And yet intimate companionship is established on a longer timescale than the capacity to give and receive pleasure or warm emotions. This intimate companionship depends in substantial part on our capacity to take into account what is good for the other in the long term. Otherwise we soon reap the fruits of earlier mistaken choices. What, then, if it is not possible to trust another but a bond has resulted? Such a relation is too weak to bear what the future will bring.

There is a nobility in our human nature that contrasts with what is to be found simply in fulfilling our appetites in the here and now. Tobias and Sarah retained this connection to the future. Pope John Paul II observed that they end their prayer with the words: 'allow us to live together to a happy old age'. They related to each other in light of this awareness, and not only in light of their mutual attractiveness. Sex education that simply encourages young people to go off and make their own choices leads to misery rather than a lifetime of fulfillment.

Faith in God is reasonable

Sexuality here has opened out onto a vast territory of what is good. We can characterise much of this territory by saying that it is terrain over which we do not have complete control. There are things here that come to us as it were from another, as in the birth of a child or the generosity of a spouse. Who can guarantee that any couple will be able to conceive a child? A significant part of sex education is to learn to value those things that lie beyond what immediately hits our senses.

These characteristics of our sexuality all point to another party, to God. Through our sexuality we are able to experience a profound union with another person. But we can realise that such a union does not fully satisfy us – we were each made for something greater. It is a reasonable faith that sees in our sexuality the sign of an even more complete union with God. To what extent in sex education are we able to convey to our young people the depths of our humanity? If even an enchanting and enduring union with another does not completely satisfy, is it not reasonable to conclude that there is a yet more profound union to which we are called?

A basis for making choices

One might think that human frailty and the consequences of original sin mean that we cannot expect our sons and daughters actually to find what is most satisfying. But the first step is to be able to see that some things lead to life, while other things lead to misery. We need a clear basis for making our choices. The philosopher Charles Taylor identifies this quite directly in his book, *Sources of the Self,* as amongst the most fundamental of all issues at stake in the modern world. In throwing out moral codes we lose a critical source of our capacity to choose what is good.

The sixth and ninth commandments in this case are at the heart of the moral code: 'You shall not commit adultery'; 'You shall not covet your neighbour's spouse.' The reality is that we each have a tendency to sin, and often desire what is wrong or likely to lead to our own harm. The Church teaches that *all* taking of sexual pleasure outside of a marriage is wrong.[33] This is true both for the passionate kiss between a boyfriend and girlfriend, as also for full-scale adultery. This might seem a little excessive, but it is obvious that sexual activity is wider than intercourse. After all, you can transmit STDs through oral sex, mutual masturbation or even heavy petting. The taking of mutual sexual pleasure evidently does unite, as the operation of oxytocin and vasopressin give consistent witness. Clear boundaries are a central feature of a moral code, in representing as they do underlying realities that are actually present. To bond with another, and yet not be in a place to bond at the level which brings an enduring satisfaction, is to side with Esau rather than Jacob. One quickly learns to value one's own sensual satisfactions above one's own genuine good and the good of others.

And yet we need to do more than just offer a moral code at this point in history. A moral code quickly becomes empty if it is not explicitly confirmed by one's own experience. Each young person needs experience of their own that does indeed indicate that life is more secure when grounded in the good of others, rather than when focused on their own sensual pleasure. Pleasure is not denied us as a result, but intensified for the longer term. Love takes into account the destiny of the other: 'The greater the feeling of responsibility for the person, the more true love there is.'[34]

Sex education completed by an angel

And what else about the story of Tobit? An angel guided Tobias in his choice of a wife. What we see here is sex education completed by an angel! Tobias was accompanied by the angel Raphael on his journey to rescue his father's silver. Raphael it was who advised Tobias to marry Sarah and who bound the demon. God's intervention was needed for Tobias and Sarah to enter into a mature understanding of their sexuality. How else could they flourish in a fallen world? And, indeed, Pope John Paul II taught that Tobias and Sarah's relationship represents an image of life in the beginning, before sin entered the world.

It is not as if we have to select from these goods things linked to our sexuality as from amongst a cold set of things that are 'good for us'. God holds out good things to us throughout our lives, and moves our hearts towards them as circumstances unfold. The sacrament of reconciliation, confession, can also play a role. It is a precious gift to help your children acquire this habit through its regular experience. God's grace is then there to help them navigate the trials that they will encounter in life. The practice of our faith is not some luxury that has only a marginal effect on life: effective sex education is only possible when God acts in our favour as well.

And if this is true for young people who are learning to express their sexuality in a way that brings a lifetime of fulfillment, then it is also true for parents as well. Prayer for our children must be part of our determination as parents, reflecting the strength of our desire. It may be the case that husband and wife are not united on these matters, and that only one is willing to take a clear stand. One mother asked her husband whether he would be willing to say a single Hail Mary for their children with her each night. If this is an area that you want to tackle with determination, then means will be found.

God gives grace to parents to carry out their mission to educate their children: 'In granting married persons the privilege and great responsibility of becoming parents, God gives them the grace to carry out their mission adequately.'[35] We need to subject our choices to the path that God has revealed to his Church, and to the inspirations of the Holy Spirit.

Heart to heart

Sex education is effective when it springs from the heart. This is Blessed John Henry Newman's phrase 'cor ad cor loquitur' – heart speaks unto heart. We can expect the hearts of our sons and daughters to seek what is good only when we act from the deepest desires of our own hearts for their good. We must set our hearts on what is good for our children, and give expression to these desires in the very fabric of our lives and choices. As parents we cannot simply hand this task over to others. Effective sex education is uncompromising in engaging the entire person and life of the parent.

Resources

Author's note: Parents will need to apply their own judgment in making use of these resources. Inclusion in this list is not intended as a form of endorsement for every aspect or claim.

Materials to inform parents

Books

Anderson, C. and Granados, J., 2009, *Called to love: approaching John Paul II's theology of the body*, Doubleday.

Butler, B., Evert, J. and Evert, C., 2008, *Theology of the body for teens: parent's guide*, Ascension Press.

Fitch, J.T., 2005, *Questions kids ask about sex*, Revell.

Grossman, M., 2009, *You're teaching my child what? A physician exposes the lies of sex education and how they harm your child*, Regnery Publishing.

McIlhaney, J.S., and Bush, F.M., 2008. *Hooked: new science on how casual sex is affecting our children*, Moody Publishers.

Morrow, T.G., 2003, *Christian courtship in an over sexed world*, Our Sunday Visitor.

Nerbun, A., Taylor, R. and Hogan, R., 1991, *Our power to love: God's gift of our sexuality*, Ignatius Press.

Pontifical Council for the Family, 1995, *The truth and meaning of human sexuality: guidelines for education within the family*, Vatican City.

Sattler, H.V. (Fr.), 2009, *Parents, children and the facts of life*, Tan.

Scherrer, C. and B., 1997, *The joyful mysteries of life*, Ignatius Press.

Stepp, Larua, 2007, *Unhooked: how young women pursue sex, delay love and lose at both*, Riverhead Books.

Websites and organisations

www.americancollegeofpediatricians.org/Abstinence-Education. html – Advice from the American College of Pediatricians on abstinence-until-marriage sex education.

www.catholiceducation.org – The section of this website on sexuality offers a range of informative articles on Catholic approaches to sexuality.

www.famyouth.org.uk – Family Education Trust website offers a range of publications designed to support the role of a parent in offering sex education to their sons and daughters, including *Too much, too soon* and *Waking up to the morning after pill*.

www.medinstitute.org/ – Resources and comment from the Medical Institute, "Sexual Health for Life", the organisation behind the book *Hooked*.

www.pureloveclub.com – Resources and contacts related to the theology of the body, including how to establish a group to support chastity.

www.woomb.org – offers a range of resources and information on natural family planning.

www.thetheologyofthebody.com/ – resources on the Pope John Paul's Theology of the Body for younger people and parents.

Materials for parents to discuss with young people (as appropriate)

Alive to the World, books on character development for use in school or in the home (published by Gracewing), with additional downloads which help parents teach their children about sex. See www.alivetotheworld.co.uk.

Bevere, L., 2002, *Kissed the girls and made them cry: why women lose when they give in*, Trust Media Distribution.

Butler, B. Evert, J. and Evert, C., 2006, *Theology of the body for teens: student workbook*, Ascension Press.

Lennart Nillson's classic photos of life in the womb – *A Child is Born* (Life Delta, 2004) and *Life* (Abrams, 2006), although some selectivity or discussion may be required in any use with young people.

This is my body, Philos Educational Publishing. [Online, accessed May 2011], http://thisismybody.co.uk/ This programme is intended for use schools with young people aged 10-11, with sex education addressed by parents in the home; parents are able to borrow the resource by contacting the publishers.

Wetzel, R., 2009, *Sexual wisdom: a guide for parents, young adults, educators, and physicians*. [Online, accessed May 2011], http://www.sexualwisdom.com/16-17book.html, Sex Education for Advanced Beginners, Inc. A home-based course of sex education for older teenagers, endorsed by the Pontifical Council for the Family.

51

Endnotes

Pontifical Council for the Family, 1995, *The truth and meaning of human sexuality: guidelines for education within the family*, Vatican City, §23.

[2] Hanley, M., 2011, *Catholic Church & the Global AIDS Crisis*, Catholic Truth Society.

[3] Waite, L.J. & Gallagher, M., 2001, *The case for marriage: why married people are happier, healthier, and better off financially*, Broadway Books.

[4] Hallfors, D.D. et al., 2004, Adolescent depression and suicide risk: Association with sex and drug behaviour, *American Journal of Preventive Medicine*, 27(3), 224-231.

[5] Brizendine, L., 2006, *The female brain*, Morgan Road Books.

[6] McIlhaney, J.S., Jr & Bush, F.M., 2008, *Hooked: new science on how casual sex is affecting our children*, Moody Publishers, p82.

[7] Uvnäs-Moberg, K., 1998, Oxytocin may mediate the benefits of positive social interaction and emotions, Psychoneuroendocrinology, 23(8), 819–835. Fisher, H., 2005, *Why we love: The nature and chemistry of romantic love*, Holt Paperbacks.

[8] Brizendine, L., 2006, *The female brain*, Morgan Road Books.

[9] *Catechism of the Catholic Church*, 2337.

[10] Stets, J.E., 1991, Cohabiting and Marital Aggression: The Role of Social Isolation, *Journal of Marriage and the Family* 53, 669-680

[11] Robins, L. and Reiger, D., 1990, *Psychiatric Disorders in America*, Free Press, p. 72.

[12] Clarkberg, M., Stolzenberg, R.M. & Waite, L.J., 1995, Attitudes, values, and entrance into cohabitational versus marital unions. *Social Forces*, 74(2), 609–632.

[13] Pontifical Council for the Family, 1995, *The truth and meaning of human sexuality: guidelines for education within the family*, Vatican City, §20.

[14] Sacred Congregation For Catholic Education, 1983, *Educational Guidance In Human Love: Outlines for sex education*, Vatican City, §32.

[15] Pontifical Council for the Family, 1995, *The truth and meaning of human sexuality: guidelines for education within the family*, Vatican City, §78.

[16] Pontifical Council for the Family, 1995, *The truth and meaning of human sexuality: guidelines for education within the family*, Vatican City, §66.

[17] Pontifical Council for the Family, 1995, *The truth and meaning of human sexuality: guidelines for education within the family*, Vatican City, Vatican City, §129.

[18] Papadopoulos, L., 2010, *Sexualisation of young people review*, The Home Office.

[19] Internet Pornography Statistics, 2011, www.internet-filter-review. toptenreviews.com/internet-pornography-statistics-pg5.html [Online, accessed 3rd January 2011].

[20] Pokorny, S., 2010, *On The Road to Freedom*, www.tobinstitute.org/page.a csp?ContentID=96, [Online, accessed 17th August 2010].

[21] Pontifical Council for the Family, 1995, *The truth and meaning of human sexuality: guidelines for education within the family*, Vatican City, §146.

[22] Pontifical Council for the Family, 1995, *The truth and meaning of human sexuality: guidelines for education within the family*, Vatican City, §65, §66, §75.

[23] Pontifical Council for the Family, 1995, *The truth and meaning of human sexuality: guidelines for education within the family*, Vatican City, §133.

[24] Pontifical Council for the Family, 1995, *The truth and meaning of human sexuality: guidelines for education within the family*, Vatican City, §127.

[25] Pontifical Council for the Family, 1995, *The truth and meaning of human sexuality: guidelines for education within the family*, Vatican City, §126-7.

[26] Sheeran, P. and Taylor, S., 1999, Predicting intentions to use condoms: a meta-analysis and comparison of the theories of reasoned action and planned behaviour, *Journal of Applied Social Psychology*, 29: 1624–1675

[27] Richens, J., Imrie, J. & Copas, A., 2000, Condoms and seat belts: the parallels and the lessons, *Lancet*, 400–403.

[28] Glasier, A., 2006, Editorial: Emergency contraception, *British Medical Journal*, 333 (7568), 560–561.

Pontifical Council for the Family, 1995, *The truth and meaning of human sexuality: guidelines for education within the family*, Vatican City, §146.

[30] Canons 1329, 1398: cf. *Catechism of the Catholic Church*, 2272.

[31] Stammers, T., 2007, 'Sexual health in adolescents: Saved sex and parental involvement are key to improving outcomes', *British Medical Journal-International Edition*, 334 (7585), 103–103.

[32] McNeely C. et al, 2002, Mother's influence on the timing of first sex among 14 and 15 year-olds, *Journal of Adolescent Health* 31:256-65; Blake, S. et al, 2001, Effects of parent-child communications intervention on young adolescents' risk for early sexual intercourse, *Family Planning Perspectives*, 33:52-61.

[33] *Catechism of the Catholic Church*, 2351-2.

[34] Pope John Paul II, 1993, *Love and responsibility*, Ignatius Press.

[35] Pontifical Council for the Family, 1995, *The truth and meaning of human sexuality: guidelines for education within the family*, Vatican City, §37.

The Role of Christian Grandparents

We live in a time of constant change, when the latest fashions and technology dominate popular culture, and society seems to be moving further away from God. Yet the role of grandparents – in a society where life expectancy is growing, and often both parents work – is becoming stronger. This booklet explores how grandparents can be present in the lives of their grandchildren to pass on the wisdom they have gained and the faith they have received.

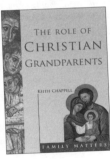

Keith Chappell studied at the Maryvale Institute in Birmingham and Oxford University, teaches theology and works as a family mediator. He lives in Berkshire with his wife Maeve and their two children.

ISBN: 978 1 86082 635 1

CTS Code: PA 15

Lumen

The Catholic Gift to Civilisation

In a recent debate, broadcast worldwide by the BBC, over 87% of the audience rejected the motion that the Catholic Church is a force for good in the world. To set the record straight, this booklet summarises the extraordinary fruitfulness of the faith, noting that our university system, art, music, legal tradition, charity and even much of our science arises from Catholic civilisation and Catholic minds. Besides encouraging Catholics, this booklet will be of great interest to teachers and general enquirers of some faith or none.

Fr Marcus Holden is parish priest of Ramsgate and Minster, Southwark, and course tutor and writer for the Maryvale Institute's M.A. in Apologetics.

Fr Andrew Pinsent is a priest of the diocese of Arundel and Brighton and Research Director of the Ian Ramsey Centre for Science and Religion at Oxford University. He was formerly a particle physicist at CERN.

ISBN: 978 1 86082 725 9

CTS Code: EV 6